CITY

of

RIVERS

CITY

of

RIVERS

ZUBAIR AHMED

McSWEENEY'S
POETRY SERIES

MᶜSWEENEY'S
SAN FRANCISCO

www.mcsweeneys.net

Copyright © 2012 Zubair Ahmed

Cover art by Saelee Oh
This book was typeset in Fournier.

The McSweeney's Poetry Series is edited by
Dominic Luxford and Jesse Nathan.

McSweeney's and colophon are registered trademarks of McSweeney's,
a privately held company with wildy fluctuating resources.

Printed in Michigan by Thomson-Shore

ISBN: 978-1-938073-02-1

CONTENTS

MEASURING THE STRENGTH OF A SPARROW'S THIGH

I've been walking for many nights now,
Heading south in Bangladesh
Where the sea churns
Into a hundred deltas
And the landscape looks like a rotting nail.
There's a dead sparrow
In my right pocket,
And in my left pocket a map given to me
By my great-grandmother,
A map of my country when it was not
My country—East Bengal, East Pakistan.
I'm wearing my father's jacket.
He was a man
Stronger than the ghosts in his bones.
My shoes are cotton.
My mother knit them one evening
As she stared at our cat
Which had swelled
To three times its usual size.
I thought our cat was lucky.
My mother left its corpse exactly
Where it died, on the dresser, beneath
The mirror.
When I was young
My brother became a mountain, always closer
To the sky than me,
Always large in the distance

Growing larger as I drew nearer.
I am wearing his shirt—
It hangs loose
Like the rings of Saturn.

A FIELD OF WELLS

My great-grandmother left
Before the sun rose
To gather water from a field of wells
Seventeen miles north.
I watched from my bed
As she kneeled in the corner
And bathed her arms with dust.
I think she prayed.
She opened the door,
Careful not to waken the crickets
Sleeping within us.
Before she left, her face forgot
Our names.
Today, the Ganges will be dense
With dead bodies.

ASHULIA

For seven years
My father drove me to Ashulia every evening
To watch the sunset.
Back then, Ashulia was nothing,
A long stretch of dirt road
Cutting through a wide river
Which passed us on both sides
Like someone lost within us.
I remember his gray hair,
His missing teeth and spotted skin.
His laughter gave birth to the softness of my skull
And the uneven beating of my heart.
He told me to fold a muslin sari,
Throw it into the river
And watch it float away.
I asked him about God,
Under which rock he hides his mansion.
He told me he found God
On the corner of his cigarette.
Twenty years later, his body floated
Through all two-hundred-fourteen rivers of Bangladesh.

My Ghost Sits in a Chair
Near the Jamuna River

His face looks
Like an animal stretched by pulleys.
He must be the type who knows
The value of a bent needle
Placed on the coffin of a weaver.

Stars

As a boy, I accidentally
Set myself on fire
Under the stars.

I stood in the dark orchard
With a different weight,
Glowing among the guavas
I couldn't eat.

I became a goat
Chewing on the same blade of grass
For decades,
Knowing the desert
Can never be eaten.

GARDEN

I turn on
All the lights in our apartment.
It makes my mom's garden
Look like the Amazon.
My father's pills
Glow like cadavers,
My brother's comic books like salted slugs,
The ceiling like a chapel.

We never turn on all the lights,
Only the one in the kitchen
So my mom can cook.
My dad watches television
In the dark.
My brother sleeps all day.

I will leave again tomorrow.
For now, I turn on
All the lights in our apartment
In these late, last hours.

A DOG IN BANGLADESH

My tired body
Under the white sun.

A child half-buried in the ground.

Bermuda grass grows in the corners of my room—
An invasion of Bangladesh by grass!
The pictures on my wall expire like dying birds.

A dog is drowning in the drains of Rayarbazaar.
Should I save it?
Its legs are broken
Like the chair I sleep in.

A Road to the Sky

Vultures eating the meat of freshly buried men.
All the good men are buried.
Children sell knives at the corner,
A raven pretends to be a crow,
Taxis drive through the streets
Narrow as blood vessels.
Inside a gray building of Rayarbazaar
A woman injects herself with cow blood
And places a bet on which chicken
Will survive longest under water.

No Light on the Hilltop

My right leg walks off
Alone
And finds itself
Among the vines that ruin houses,
Among the sand that spied on my childhood.
My right leg wanders
Through the skeletons of couches, abandoned carpets,
Drawing rooms, and ash.
My right leg looks toward the hilltop.
My left leg will never make it there.

SHAVING

I cut myself while shaving
And see my grandfather in the blood,
The man responsible
For the worms
In my garden.
The sound of a river
Enters the room.
The water smells of downed power lines
And the frozen bones of the morning.
Through the window I see
The sky eating birds,
And inside my shoulders I feel a dead horse.

SELF-PORTRAIT WITH GLASS BOTTLE AND KITE

I've spent so many years
With the glass bottle my uncle gave me
During a barbecue
In the monsoon rains.
That day we ate burgers soggy
With curry sauce,
Debated Saeed Anwar's batting form
And wondered which cinema hall
Would be bombed next.

My father gave me a kite
When I was three.
It looked like the Great Barrier Reef of Australia.
My mother made it
From the woven threads of jute.
I learned how to fly
On the summer winds
Of Dhaka.

Now, sitting on a bench
At Joe Pool Lake
In Cedar Hill, Texas,
I watch the birds
Dismantle my kite.
This glass bottle is clear
As the mountains I imagine on the horizon.

I've seen bones rain down
From this Texas sky.
I remember the bloodstained windows
That gave birth to my country.

4 A.M.

You go outside,
Place your body
Deep inside the darkness
And wait for snow.
You wear the skin
Of a defeated man.
A piece of moon
Falls into your hands,
Secretly poisonous
Like the flowers
Of a potato plant.

At a Photo Exhibition
for the 1971 Liberation War

It was an ordinary day—
The crows scavenging for cow guts,
The beggar at his usual corner
Still missing an eye.
This day thirty years ago
Bangladesh defeated Pakistan.
At the exhibit, I saw a picture of a boy
Whose four limbs and face
Were cut off.
A dog was eating his torso.
In his eyes I saw
A field waiting in moonlight,
A village burning in the center,
His mother walking naked into the river.
When I sleep I join the dead
In vast courtyards.
We wait for buses and trains
That arrive exactly on time
But have no windows.

AYON

I found a picture of you
Standing on the roof,
Hands crossed behind your back,
Body facing
The black sky.
It was a hot night.
You talked about your mother's death
Softly, as if she'd hear you
Saying something wrong.
You told me you believed
You were becoming the strokes of a boatman
Crossing the Brahmaputra at dawn,
His hands moving up and down,
Trying to become water
And failing.
You smiled and believed
That your eyes would refuse
To let light in.
You believed a small breeze,
Small like a child's coffin,
Would prove your body was made of moths.
And all you believed
Happened.

Ten years later, I look at your picture
And can only think of rain
Falling over Dhaka,

Flooding every street,
Even the ones that go nowhere,
Flooding the now-empty roof
Where an old song is slowly ending.

BONFIRE AT 3 A.M.

We walk down into the dry lake bed
Holding bottles and a bag of wood.

The ground crumbles under the weight of starlight.
We start a bonfire.

I look at this girl who came along.
She smiles at me,

Standing like a redwood
Scorched by wildfire,

A fragment of my dead sister.

She holds my arm.
I moan like my father's whip.

CATACOMBS

The stones here throb like my mother's left earring
And reek of flowers.
The moon watches through the walls,
A rat chews on a golden watch.
I walk these hallways with an arrow in my tongue,
My skull wrapped neatly in satin.

WE'RE ALMOST THERE

I'm sitting beside a sleeping man and a dead man
On this bus heading north.

Outside I see the disappearing forests of Bangladesh
And the gray fingers of my father.

The seats smell like black snow.

GONE OFF ALONE

I heard your windshield crack
In a dream.

The washing machine churns
With stained bed sheets.

I lean forward, and listen
To the graying of my hair.

I Am Inside the Mind of a Scientist

Past the leather factories by the river
Toward the foreclosed homes
I entered a house
And faced a dead man
As black as the trees around us,
His chin held high, shirt tucked in,
Nose half clipped.
I took a hair sample from behind his right ear
And burned it.
It burned blue,
The color the sky used to be.

I study his shadow,
Angled seventy-seven degrees from the horizontal.
The light source is somewhere beyond
The years of my life.

THE FOREST COYOTES OF MY COUNTRY

I wander the woods
By Cox's Bazaar
Like a coyote

Lost among the trees,
Almost hungry,
Almost alone.

Night seeps
Through the branches.
I am the animal that places a stone
In each ear of the dead

Who are now too heavy
For the stars to carry.

It's Raining Again

And the old man sitting on the stairs
Is still sitting on the stairs
Wearing a leathered face.
A rickshaw puller tries to light a wet cigarette.
A dog in the corner drinks the overflow.
Entire alleyways are stripped of color.
Nearby, a river begins its migration
To the fields and homes
Where people sit without clothing.
They whisper about disease,
About the acceptable ways
Of burying their children.

THE GIFT

Eighteen years ago I gave you what I thought was a piece of diamond. Why did you give it back to me in your will?

I WATCH THE SHADOWS OF BIRDS WAKING AT DAWN TO PICK THE WORMS CLEAN

I know what the day holds—
Organizing bottles of fish oil on my shelves,
Feeding the spider in my keyhole three poppy seeds,
Reading letters addressed to the old tenant
Who lived in my apartment years ago, and now
Wanders the forests of New Zealand
Like a bird of paradise.
The sun is gray.
Children gather at bus stops, their faces covered with black boxes.
When school starts, the principal will announce, in a voice
Resembling the thirty-second window of the Empire State Building,
The chores of the day
And the students will line up in their white shirts and khaki pants
Ready to write about the secret lives of sparrows.
I once went to school on days like this.

On a cold summer morning, I visited the hallways
That tried so hard to align the veins in my body.
I felt the doors and the columns, worn on the inside.
I stared at the ceiling, which still hung
Like a boy hanging off the side of a cliff,
Not calling for help because he knows
He's truly alone.

As dusk arrives, I will think of a friend, Iftekhar,
And his river-sized shoulders.
We used to play soccer in the monsoon rains.

Through my windows I can see acres of fields
Lying in the ruins of the wind.
I will offer these fields bottles of fish oil.
I will wait till night falls and I can't see
The shadows of birds surrounding me.

REACHING HALF-LIFE IN MY BACKYARD

The clouds move quickly over these slums
But it rarely stops raining.
My chair digs into the mud,
Bushes and weeds creep through the fence.
The vastness of the sky resembles a cup of fresh water
Floating in the sea.

I forget everyone—
Cousins, brothers, elders, friends.
I forget the shape
Of my brother's hand,
The smell of my mother's clothes.
I feel my father slip
Deeper into his coffin.

I've spent half my life sitting here
Drinking the monsoon rains.
One evening I saw the sky turn a dark green,
The same color I saw the day I fell in love
With everything around me,
The same day I lost everything I'd loved before then.

A Few Words to My Father

Water, pills, gates.

Smoke rushing
Into the stony channels
Of your chest.

The sandals on your feet
Gather moss.

Your eyes
Are the color of limestone
After years of rain.

Nothing I do
Will change anything.

On the Night Train to Munich,
the Spirit Asks Me a Simple Question

Yellow.
All the lights here
Are yellow,
Dead and slow,
Trying to make each town we pass
Their home.
The man beside me talks in his sleep.
I don't understand him
But I hear needles in his voice.
Maybe he thinks
He is dying on this train
From a disease only he
Believes in
And is now saying a prayer to God.
Maybe he lost his God
And wants nothing
On this train.
Outside, the moonlight falls
On boarded shops,
Trees stripped naked,
Streets as empty as my grandmother's eyes
As her bones whiten too early.
I close my eyes
And see a blind man
Begging on the corner,
The shape of a leather factory
Towering behind him.

My seven-year-old eyes
Could have watched him die
And felt no pity.
But on this train to Munich
I am made only of grass,
My body spread thin
Along the colored banks
Of the Brahmaputra River.
Soon, I will grow old.
The railroad will sing.
My breath
Will turn to snow
And fall over
My family cemetery.

No One

No one fears the minutes before midnight
When you lie in bed counting the stars
Through cracks in the roof,
Or the soil that makes you age
Two days at a time.
No one fears the smell of prom,
Future thieves and Nobel Laureates
Dancing faster and faster
As the night grows long
As the thread I tied to my mother's hair
On the night she died.
My date couldn't stop talking
About the vein on her forehead
That couldn't be hidden with makeup.
No one fears the breath of the dead,
And no one listens to my country's flag.
No one listens to the head
Hanging from the tree in my backyard,
Even when it sings beautifully
And the birds gather to listen. No one listens
To the twelve-year-old boy at the rail yard
Who hopes the train's wheels are round enough
To take him beyond the mountains.
No one fears the scorpions on my shoulder.
No one fears the northern winds
Off the Himalayas
Mixing with the damp air of Dhaka,

Giving birth to water that isn't rain or snow
Floating above graying trees.
No one listens to the city anymore,
I roam the streets like a man tired
From drinking too much dust.

POWER

The light in the tunnel
Is turned off
To save electricity.
A door is left open in anger.
Inside the darkness
Hang miles and miles
Of wire
Extending
Out of my father's chest.

RAYARBAZAAR

My thoughts stroll
Through the alleys of Rayarbazaar.
Sleep stains the walls here.
The mud-streaked sky.
Even the dogs look tired.
A widow confesses her sins
To a broken wheel.
My thoughts walk
Through the streets of Rayarbazaar.
I drink from a bucket of dead mosquitoes.

I Once Held a Quail and Stared into Its Eyes for Eleven Minutes

I sit on the roof
Looking at a storm in the north.

Yesterday I placed an urn
On the dinner table
Twenty minutes
Before our guests arrived.

My family debated why
I put it there—
Maybe to mourn the death
Of my auntie, shot
In the head by a wild man.
Maybe
Because I stopped spending time
Sitting in the trees
Of our backyard.

I once shot a rifle into the sky
Blindly
And hit a hawk
In the neck.
He fell like a brown arrow
Launched from some celestial city.
When I removed the bullet
Blood streamed down my arms—
The dark water
Beneath the Atlantic.

Three days later, the hawk flew away.
I wonder if I could have poured
His strength into the mold
Of a man
And discovered immortality,
Or a secret death.

The storm draws nearer.

I Close My Eyes and Find Myself in the Exact Center of Dhaka

Tell me why the sky is above
And not under our bodies.
The skin of men spread so thin
The world becomes transparent.
The minerals every doctor searches for
Hidden beneath the feet
Of Bangla farmers.
Kidnapped children packed in trucks
Dry in the sun,
Women line up
To let their organs
Be harvested for medicine.
I don't understand anything anymore—
The moon walking away from us
Because we're discovering
Who we really are.

Sajeed, Who Lost Four Fingers for Lying

In his sleep
Someone poured glue
In his eyes.
Sajeed woke up and whispered
"Thank you."

As I Walk in Armstrong Park at 4:13 a.m.

The lights flicker.
A giant wooden castle stands
In the middle of the park
Surrounded by sand.
By the corner, swings
Sway by themselves.

The air inside me whispers.
I hear someone talking about a past
In which this patch of land floated
In the sky.

On April 21, 1856, a cowboy lassoed it down
And called it Duncanville.
That night, lying under the stars,
He froze to death.
Only the emptiness here
Remembers him.

MINYARD'S

I'm buying groceries:
Chicken breast, potatoes,
Three yellow onions.
Cops in the parking lot
Make racist jokes.
A tomato I pick up
Understands why
My body is a cloud.

WE ALL GATHER TO EAT AND
WATCH TELEVISION

My grandparents, cousins, brother, and sisters
Gather to eat dinner and watch *Hercules*.
I pick the bones from my fish, take a sip of lassi.
In the corner are photos taken
With shaky hands long before my birth.
Everyone's laughing. The room is filled with age,
Dry skin, oiled hair, unbrushed teeth.
Hercules picks up a rock and crushes a head
Of the Hydra, and my grandfather laughs
Like he did when my uncle, wounded and broken
In the Liberation War of 1971,
Came back with a head full of hair.
When he laughs, everyone joins him.
My cousin hits his sister
Pretending she is the Hydra.
She starts to cry, but no one notices.
My uncles discuss politics as Hercules disagrees
With Hera. They smile quietly and talk in detail
About the pieces of Khaled that were discovered in plastic bags
Outside the Parliament building.
They wonder whether they should have let
The dogs continue eating.
Another auntie joins in, the one who abandoned her son
In the monsoon rains of 1999 at the corner of Sher-e-Bangla Road,
Where dogs are killed and dumped. She was mad at her husband
For not making enough money.
The years have carved an emptiness in her face.

My mother serves me more fish and asks
How I like it. I look up at her and smile, as I always do.
The monsoon rains begin tomorrow, and mark the beginning
Of nothing special.

TO A FRIEND

I am zero point nine-zeroes six six gigainches tall.
According to the equation we derived as children
I'd grow at the rate of Dhaka's population.
Scientists are wrong about the weight of light.
It is exactly one-hundred-thirty-two-point-three kilograms,
The weight of a ripened guava.
All those times we'd stay up till sunrise
Under our schoolyard guava trees
Eating guavas under the summer skies of Dhaka,
We were eating light.
You once told me the economy operates
On a sine wave.
And it does, according to O-Level Economics.
But we were just demagnetized iron bars
Dreaming of facing north with complete certainty.
Lately, I've seen landslides in the twilight.
I've seen streams of blackened water,
Sad smoke rising from the structures of economies,
Wingless birds whose feathers are ice.
Standing on a heap of garbage, miles of dead computers,
Rusted cars, and abandoned blenders.
But I've also had the fun of drilling
Through mountains with a screwdriver,
Cutting through stainless steel with plasma,
And drinking from lakes seventeen-thousand feet high.
I wish you could see how blue a light wave
Of four-hundred-seventy-five nanometers can be.

When I solved
A thirteen-step differential equation in twelve steps,
I thought of you.
I wish you had eaten the food I cooked
On top of Mount Everest using a stove with striking similarities
To the mud stoves we made as children.

I ONCE BELIEVED I WAS A MAN OF SCIENCE

Where do you think such beliefs go
After they're abandoned?
The line I drew
Has become a horse
In some other world.
A gray horse
The exact shade of my grandfather's hair.

THE FIELDS OF AGA KHAN, SUMMER 2004

The nights are never cold here,
Just starless as the blanket
My great-grandmother died under,
Its thread forged by the breeze
That carries my skull into the sky.
I long for a road dark from rain,
A road that ends inside a forest
And goes up into the clouds
Or down into a secret well.
In the slow hours of the night
The grass will grow a thousand feet tall.

CLASSROOM

This white classroom
Reminds me of my mother's face
Locked in a bottle I threw
Into a landfill by the Ganges.
On the windowsill
There is a dead hummingbird,
Its wing beautifully twisted.
I am a home
For my strangled bones.

You

Why are you worried
About the silk threads
Hanging from my wounds?

Why are you so concerned
About the grass
Growing under our house?

Don't be troubled
By the ancient ropes
That carried
The bodies of my ancestors

Or the silver light
That shines through my past,
The speeches of insects,
The trees taking root
In the smallest muscles of my head.

The Crow's Ghost Watches

1.

Today begins seven months
Of monsoon rains.
Cloud shadows
Cover the streets.
A dog eats
The corpse of a crow.
I have nothing to do today, like every day,
So I count the number of times
The dog looks up at me.
When the rains begin
The taxi with the sweaty driver,
Whose pregnant wife has left him,
Will crush the dog's head.

No one will notice.
People will pretend the smell comes from the gardens
That were once everywhere.
And those who remember the war of 1971 will be relieved
To find it is a dog's cadaver.

My father tells me stories—
How the sound of blood is etched
Into his eardrums, how he has lost the will to dream
And the ability to listen carefully.

I hear stories of how I was almost not born,
How my two-year-old mother was left by a pond
(By accident or intention, that's a secret)
Where a soldier found her
And instead of shooting her
In each eye
He left her on a porch facing the red Meghna River.
I believe I am the unborn son of this river,
For it repaired the broken muscle
Of my mother's heart.

2.

Soon, twilight will roam the white streets of Berlin
And I will try to remember again
Where I come from.
Wherever I go, the sparrows look the same—
Small songs that have lost their meanings.
The sky looks like the dark glass
Of an abandoned home.
People have faces
Shaped like empty riverbeds.
At dawn, I wake up somewhere new.

3.

The crow's ghost speaks:
When I was young, every street was a forest
Filled with birches white as the first snows of winter,
A forest where you can hear
The reasons you exist,
And the reasons
You shouldn't.

INVENTORY

If I count
All my bones and organs,
All my hairs and eyelashes,
My fingers and teeth,
I don't end up with a number
But an image of morning
When the curtains
Are heavy with dust.
My shoulders are heavy and worn.
My skin is a carpet
Abandoned in the street.
This December, I could have returned home.
Instead, I chose to stand by the Pacific.
I'm driving a car in the forest at night
And the trees are dressed
In my grandmother's shawls.

I Step into My
Car on a Sunday Night

When the light retreats
Into homes, I pretend to be
The only man alive.
I become the animal so close
To extinction it finds peace.
I am not alone.
I have a mother, sitting
On the chair I made
For her 45th birthday.
I have a brother, studying
In an art institute to become
A graphic designer.
And I have a father, dark,
Bent, liquid.
This was twenty years ago—
I think I still have them.

I start my car, drive south
Until I hit a street
That may or may not exist.

THE WATER OF LAKE TAHOE

The sound of water repairs my skin.
I stand inside the wind,
Breathing in the tips of waves
And the branches coated
In pre-dawn ice.
I'm afraid to go anywhere.
I'm afraid of the empty rooms
That await me,
The photos on my table
That must be sorted,
The heaps of paper being folded
By the ghosts who refuse to haunt me.

A PRAYER

I'm stronger than the memory of sand
Hidden in my hands.
It will be years
Before I return home.
My bones
Are hollow as the center
Of a horseshoe—
Let me sit in them
And light a small fire.

SECOND HOME

It snowed four days ago.
I don't feel as cold
As I am supposed to.
I almost believe
I'm as strong as I need to be.
I come across a field
Wide enough to hold all
The letters I've written,
Even the ones I burned
In the cemetery.

You Are Gone, Brother

Brother,
We sprinkled the dirt from our sandals
Onto our food.
We couldn't see the stars in Dhaka,
So we invited the fireflies
To replace them.

The stench of a rotting dog
As we played cricket at dawn.
The horizon lurking
Behind the monsoon clouds,
And our bones made of sand.

We danced in sewage
And brushed our teeth with ash.

The promises we made
Wait in a bottle between two layers
Of the atmosphere.

You washed your hands
In the dead river.

As I wait for you, I carve a table
From other tables.
Where have you gone?
You sit inside a jar that holds more jars.

See what's happening?
Entire trees are vanishing
In the hallways of their own bodies.

We float like eyes stitched to the sky,
Looking for each other
In all the wrong places.

Most Pieces of a Broken Stone

1.

The space between my father and me fills
With grass and snow.
He stands in the dim light of the factory
Wearing a checkered shirt
And khaki pants.
Above him, stars
Hang on the sky like leaves.
He reaches for them
And whispers a prayer I cannot hear.
The shadows lengthen
And my father waits.

He knows I'm gone.

2.

On a cold night in Kreuzberg, Berlin,
I sit on a bench in Victoria Park
Above an old factory
With two chimneys staring at the sky
As if they are trying
To remember something.
The year is 1876—
A worker stands in the corner
Scraping calluses from his hands.

He thinks about his family
Whom he hasn't seen
In four years.
He tries to remember
Their faces.
His job today
Is to make five-hundred kilograms
Of cobblestone.

3.

The sky is starless.
I believe Berlin is made of light,
The kind that comes to you
When you hold your palms open.
I believe I can give the city
A third of my heart
And call it home.

4.

I walk through a field
Beside a small German town
And close my eyes—
I want to feel the wind
Pass through my body
And hear a German crow

Speak German with the weeds.
I've never been here before,
In the middle of this meadow
Under this gray sky
Surrounded by tall
Black trees
Whose leaves look like small hands.
I try to think of nothing.
I try to forget
Who I think I am.

TAENARIMORE

Sayem and I take off our shirts
And run into the rain
Faster than our legs allow.
We press our faces
Into the mud to show our thanks.
A bird sits on the far wall.
Its black eyes look into mine
And I smell raw leather.

TIME

I wish I had time
To take my father to the river,
To wash his feet,
To wash the sand
From his eyes.
I wish I had time to show my mother
The sunrise over the Sierra Nevada.
I wish I could know my brother.
I don't have time,
I have an illusion.
The days fall
Like stones
On a moonlit beach.

HELLO, BROTHER

I pick up an earthworm
And you shoot it with a rifle.
Mom screams at us,
But we don't listen.
She fed us expired milk this morning.
Sometimes in these Bengali summers,
When dust sticks to our skins
And the crows shit on our heads,
We bond like hydrocarbons,
Set mosquitoes on fire,
And eat berries whose names we can't remember.
We ride our bikes like metal antelopes,
Like drunken sparrows.
We play cricket under the monsoon clouds
And you bowl a perfect leg-spinner.
It starts to rain
So I shoot down a cloud.
We take it back to Mom
Who kisses our ears and pokes our eyes—
She does that.
We get ready for bed
With our usual battles,
And you fall asleep
Not knowing I slid the alarm clock
Under your pillow
Set for 3:17 A.M.

Driving at Night in Texas

My Grand Prix's engine
Knows no end.
I place my hand on the window
And feel the heartbeat of a fish
Freezing somewhere
Inside my mother.
I turn up the radio and listen
To the static.
I pass Juniper Bridge
And feel the waves on Joe Pool Lake.
In nights of rain
The lake begs for more water.
I wish the lake knew
It was man-made.

INSIDE AN ELEVATOR

The lights in the elevator
Have burnt out.
I walk in
And let the door close.
I can almost see
The mirror aging.
I am tired.
My legs
Hang
In the patriotic smog
Of Dhaka.
Today
I met a beautiful girl
On the top
Of a building.
I asked for her name
And her eyes
Almost
Looked into mine.

Collecting Bottles,
Wittenberg Train Station, Berlin

I believe that once, long ago, there was someone I called
Father.
He always walked in circles, and told me
"If you walk long enough, and believe,
You'll get to places
Only the rain can imagine."
The rivers of his eyes harden.
I still don't know
What he saw in me.

EIGHT OF US SLEEPING IN ONE ROOM

We breathe each other's breaths.
Outside, the sound of a motorcycle
Refusing to start.
An old man and a child sit in the stairwell
And smoke a cigarette.
These walls are more than walls.
Even in sleep, we stay only here.

CIVIL AIR PATROL

I drive my friend to a Civil Air Patrol meeting
On a foggy evening.
He tells me to pick him up two hours later.
Instead, I wander among a field of airplanes.

The wings of N1261D feel nothing like metal.
The propeller on N8189E hangs like a weathered chandelier.
In this field of metal birds,
I knock on the landing gear of N1146D and hear a sigh
From somewhere inside.

Later, I fly my friend home
On a paper airplane.

DESCENDING THROUGH RAIN

The airplane hums
As if it's about to sleep.
The cabin lights flicker.
An old man leaves his body.
Somewhere in my mind
I'm building a mansion of stone
With furniture found
In the landfills of my country.
The city below
Stares up at us
As our airplane turns to snow.

CONCESSION

I could sit here all night,
And chances are I will.
The moon lights the ocean on fire.
I watch the waves repeat themselves
Until they become a house
With soft lights and no furniture.
I begin to sleep.
My body is music.
I will never have a home.

ACKNOWLEDGMENTS

Many thanks to the editors of *Tin House*, *California Northern*, and the *Believer*, in which some of the poems in this book first appeared, sometimes under different titles and in earlier versions.

Several of these poems previously appeared in the chapbook *Ashulia* (Tavern Books, 2011). A broadside of "Shaving" was also published in 2011 by Tavern Books.

THANK YOU

I'm thankful for so much, I struggle to represent my gratitude. But here goes nothing.

I want to thank Dominic Luxford and Jesse Nathan for the hours they spent making my book what you read today. It wouldn't have taken this final shape without their time, voice, and feedback.

Thank you McSweeney's for publishing my first collection of poetry. Many thanks in particular to those who helped read, proof, fact-check, and otherwise assist in the creation of this book: Brian McMullen, Walter Green, Charlotte Crowe, John Babbott, Jared Hawkley, Jordan Karnes, Libby Wachtler, Charlotte Locke, and Olivia Taussig.

I would like to thank Michael McGriff, without whom I wouldn't be a poet, and Ga-Il Lee, who helped me better understand the meaning of words. I would also like to give thanks to Britta Ameel, Carl Adamshick, and Matthew Dickman for believing in my work, but more importantly, for believing in me.

But above all, I want to thank my family, my brother, and my parents. Without my family, I wouldn't be human. Without my brother, I would be a different person. And without my parents, I wouldn't exist.

Thank you, father. And thank you, mother.

I am very grateful for the life I've been given, and I look forward to great adventures in the future.

About the Author

Zubair Ahmed was born in 1988 and raised in Dhaka, Bangladesh. In 2005, his family won the Diversity Visa Lottery, which granted them the opportunity to immigrate to the US. Ahmed now studies mechanical engineering and creative writing at Stanford University. He is the author of the chapbook *Ashulia* (Tavern Books, 2011).

THE

MᶜSWEENEY'S POETRY SERIES

is founded on the idea that good poems can come in any style or form,
by poets of any age anywhere. Our goal is to seek out and publish
the best, most vital work we can find, regardless of pedigree. If it
were up to us, there'd still be poems in your morning paper—poems
that move, provoke, inspire, and delight. Till then, we'll publish
them the only way we know how: in beautiful hardcovers with
original art that reflects the writing within. These are books to own,
books to cherish, books to loan to friends only in rare circumstances.

SUBSCRIPTIONS

The McSweeney's Poetry Series subscription includes our next four
books for only $40—an average of $10 per book—shipping included.

You can sign up at:

store.mcsweeneys.net

PREVIOUS BOOKS

Love, an Index
by Rebecca Lindenberg

"An A-to-Z collection of poems
that are passionate, plainspoken,
elegiac, and lyric as they capture
the moments of a life shared."
—*Vanity Fair*

Fragile Acts
by Allan Peterson

"Like 'Brazil's undiscovered caverns
of amethyst,' Allan Peterson's
Fragile Acts is a major find."
—John Ashbery